THE OFFICIAL
MANCHESTER UNITED
ANNUAL 2004

**ADAM BOSTOCK
and SIMON DAVIES**

First published in 2003

Copyright © 2003
Manchester United Plc
Text and design copyright
© 2003 Carlton Books Limited

Manufactured and Distributed by
Carlton Books Limited
20 Mortimer Street
London W1T 3JW

A CIP catalogue of this book is available from
the British Library.

ISBN 0 233 05118 X

Project Editor: **Martin Corteel**
Project Art Director: **Darren Jordan**
Design: **Andy Jones**
Editorial: **Deborah Martin**
Photography: **John and Matthew Peters,
    Manchester United FC**
Picture Research: **Marc Glanville**
Production: **Lisa French**
Printed in Italy

Contents

The Secret Diary of Sir Alex Ferguson

Don't tell anybody, but when we were snooping around Carrington, we found Fergie's secret diary for 2002/03! Just before the Boss returned to his office, we managed to photocopy a few pages for you to read here...*

1 August 2002

It's the first day back in training after the summer break, and I can't wait to get back to work. Having spent my holidays in sunny Glasgow practising my shouting, I reckon I can go louder than ever – the lads have got a shock in store! New signing Rio Ferdinand won't know what's hit him, especially when I tell him about the secret cameras I've had installed here. From the comfort of my office I saw someone leave training early last year, but I'm still trying to work out whose Ferrari it was. I'm not regretting postponing my retirement yet. I just hope Arsene Wenger remembers our little arrangement and lets us win everything this year.

14 November 2002

Got into Carrington especially early this morning, as I wanted to see if I could beat the milkman. I did, but was gutted to see Gary and Phil Neville already here. I think they must have moved in. I told them that they're not to do that anymore, as everyone knows I'm supposed to be the first one in every day. Reading the papers I saw that the Daily Mirror have run a story saying that we'll be seventeen points behind the league leaders by mid-December, and that I'll be out of a job. I don't know why I bother talking to the press any more. David Beckham seems to enjoy it, though – he's never out of the news. I suppose it is of national importance what his hair looks like, though.

29 November 2002

I've been up to Scotland today to pick up my latest award – an Honorary Doctorate of Law from St Andrews University. I've been given quite a lot of honours in my time. Seeing as no one will ever read this, I may as well have a boast. I've got a knighthood, an OBE, three degrees, four doctorates and the freedom of the cities of Aberdeen, Glasgow and Manchester. That means that I'm allowed to graze cattle in the town square whenever I want. There's not a lot of grass in Albert Square, but I might take a couple of horses into one of the top bars nearby, The Sugar Lounge. They'll enjoy that, especially if the bar staff serve sugar cubes!

10 December 2002

We've beaten Newcastle, we've beaten Liverpool, and we've beaten Arsenal. So we're only three points behind the leaders. What's the Daily Mirror's number?

10 February 2003

The players are off on international duty, so I thought I'd take the day off. I watched a bit of TV in bed – those Teletubbies are good but I can never understand what they're saying. Then I did a bit of piano practice – I'm getting good, "Flower of Scotland" is my favourite tune – and then had a round of golf with Arsene Wenger. He kept hitting his ball into the rough, then it would miraculously reappear on the fairway. "I didn't see the incident, Alex," he kept insisting. Some things never change.

2 April 2003

The players are away again – more internationals! Still, it gives me a chance to visit my lovely horses at the stables. Some of them can run nearly as fast as Giggsy. I tried to enter Ryan in the Grand National once, but rules are rules. Besides, he wasn't very willing when I suggested a trial run around Carrington with me on his back!

31 December 2002

Yippee! It's my birthday today! I got lots of lovely presents – Lady Ferguson bought me a fancy new watch that will help me to count every second of injury time in matches. The players had a whip-round and bought me some singing lessons. Not sure what for, mind. We've got a game tomorrow, so I won't be celebrating New Year's Eve – again. I will call my old captain Steve Bruce, though, and wish him Happy Birthday. Brucie and me have always shared the same birthday, every year without fail. Never worked out how he did it.

*Actually the diary pages are made up! Did we fool you?

The Race for the

Many pundits predicted that the pursuit of the Premiership title in 2002/03 would be the most exciting race in the league's history. After four seasons of Manchester United and Arsenal fighting it out for positions one and two, Liverpool had muscled their way into it to finish second behind the Gunners in 2001/02. Now there were three other clubs who looked capable of mounting a challenge: Newcastle United, Chelsea and Everton. But how did it all end? Who were the tops, and who were the flops? Read this for a reminder …

August 2002

The Reds went head-to-head with one of their title rivals in only their second game, when they were away to Chelsea. But before that, they had to kick off the season against Premiership new-boys West Brom at Old Trafford. Nicknamed "The Baggies", the visitors had bags of energy and enthusiasm, but on one of the hottest days of the summer, they melted away in the second half when their skipper McInnes was sent off and super-sub Ole Gunnar Solskjaer scored for United.

Title rivals Chelsea proved to be a much tougher prospect six days later – they punished United's weakened defence with Zenden's goal after just three minutes! The Reds might have been missing Fabien Barthez, Gary Neville and Rio Ferdinand, but they still had big names on their scoresheet. David Beckham equalised in the first half, and Ryan Giggs did the same in the second after Zola had restored Chelsea's lead.

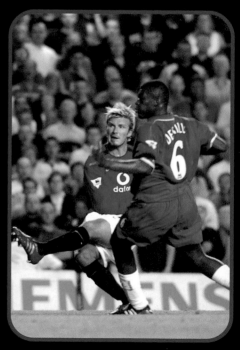

Top: **Solskjaer sinks West Brom.**

Bottom: **Beckham bags the first equaliser at Chelsea.**

Title

Celebrating Ryan's goal at Sunderland.

United travelled to the other end of the country for their next league match, but if the surroundings in Sunderland were different, the outcome was much the same – two points dropped in a score draw. Giggs scored first this time, only for Flo to equalise, but the football was largely overshadowed by Roy Keane's rumble with McAteer. The Reds captain was sent off for the injury time incident.

High Spot: Blinding goals by Beckham and Giggs in the 2–2 draw at Chelsea.
Low Spot: Keano's red card at Sunderland. He didn't play again until Christmas!

Man Utd 1–0 West Brom
17-08-2002 (Solskjaer 78)
Chelsea 2–2 Man Utd
23-08-2002 (Beckham 26, Giggs 66)
Sunderland 1–1 Man Utd
31-08-2002 (Giggs 7)

September 2002

With Fabien Barthez and record signing Rio Ferdinand back in the side, United's defence became the mean machine in September. They conceded only four goals in five games, but that couldn't stop the Reds slipping to two league defeats in a row. United's problem was clearly at the other end of the field. They were unable to score a goal in open play until the last match of the month, and had to rely on Ruud van Nistelrooy's accurate penalties to take care of Middlesbrough and then Tottenham Hotspur, both at home.

Scholes on the attack against Boro.

Between those games, United suffered embarrassing defeats to Bolton and Leeds. The Bolton result really left Fergie's men with red faces, because it was the second year in a row that the local rivals had won against all the odds at Old Trafford.

All the hype before the Leeds game was about Rio's return to Elland Road following his £30 million summer transfer, but the England defender took it all in his stride. It was just a shame that the United strikers were again off-target and unable to silence the booing home fans.

United's forwards finally got their act together for the trip to Charlton. After going 1–0 down, the Reds recovered in style with goals by Paul Scholes and Ryan Giggs from close range. Ruud had been rested to the bench, but he came on to score in the dying seconds – Solskjaer-style!

High Spot: Giggs side-stepping the goalkeeper to score at Charlton.
Low Spot: Losing 1–0 at home to Bolton for the second season in a row.

Man Utd 1–0 Middlesbro
03-09-2002 (Van Nistelrooy 28 pen.)
Man Utd 0–1 Bolton
11-09-2002
Leeds 1–0 Man Utd
14-09-2002
Man Utd 1–0 Tottenham
21-09-2002 (Van Nistelrooy 63 pen.)
Charlton 1–3 Man Utd
28-09-2002 (Scholes 54, Giggs 83, Van Nistelrooy 90)

October 2002

If United's next visitors, Everton, had made a good start to their season, their exciting teenage star Wayne Rooney was making a dream start to his football career. Fresh from scoring two goals at Wrexham in the Worthington Cup, he showed no nerves when he stepped onto the biggest stage of them all, Old Trafford.

Coming on as a sub against the Reds, the kid nicknamed Roonaldo nearly opened the scoring for the Toffees, who had stuck to their task of closing down Ruud van Nistelrooy and the other deadly Reds with great determination. But just when it seemed that Everton would escape with at least a draw, Paul Scholes scored for United – and the floodgates then opened. The ginger magician thundered in his second goal from 25 yards in injury time, moments after Ruud had tucked away his third

Quinton, Rio and Ole help shirtless Diego to celebrate his first league goal.

Premiership penalty of the season following a foul on Ole Gunnar Solskjaer by David Weir – who was unlucky to be sent off.

Unfortunately that was as good as it got for United in October. Their bid for the title faltered in the other two league games they played in a so-so month. The Reds dropped four points but it could have been much worse. They went 1–0 down in both games, and they had to face a penalty at Fulham, not long after Solskjaer had equalised. Malbranque stepped up to take it, only for Fabien Barthez to delay proceedings by kicking the mud off his studs against one post and then casually walking to the other. The referee booked Fab for time-wasting but he didn't care – he easily saved the weak shot from Malbranque.

If Fabien was the hero at Fulham, then Forlan was the man against Aston Villa when he finally scored his first Premiership goal, nine months after joining United. The Uruguayan's equalising header came just 13 minutes before time – unlucky for Villa, who'd been in the lead for almost

half the match. Diego didn't stop to sympathise, instead he raced away, pulling his shirt off in jubilant celebration.

High Spot: Forlan's first league goal for United … and the celebrations that followed it!
Low Spot: Fergie said the performance against Villa was one of the worst of the season.

Man Utd 3–0 Everton
07-10-2002 (Scholes 86, 90, van Nistelrooy 89 p)
Fulham 1–1 Man Utd
19-10-2002 (Solskjaer 62)
Man Utd 1–1 Aston Villa
26-10-2002 (Forlan 77)

Scholes scores against Everton.

The 'ginger magician' conjures up another goal.

November 2002

After breaking his Premiership duck in October, Diego scored again in November. This time his goal was even more important, turning another home draw into a last-gasp victory against Southampton. United's first goal was scored by another stranger to the scoresheet, Phil Neville. He bagged only two in the entire 2001/02 season, but one of them was also against Southampton – he's a sinner as far as the Saints are concerned!

Seven days later, the sweet smell of success turned sour for Sir Alex Ferguson's side. Playing against their legendary former goalkeeper Peter Schmeichel, United lost to Manchester City for the first time since 1989. Way back then, the score was 5–1 to the Blues and there might have been a repeat had City's strikers not wasted some good chances. Not that Kevin Keegan could complain – he was thrilled to win 3–1 against Sir Alex, who pipped him to the Premiership title in 1996, when KK was Newcastle boss.

Newcastle were later managed by one of Holland's greatest ever players, Ruud Gullit, but it was another Dutch Ruud who destroyed them at Old Trafford in November 2002. Van Nistelrooy banged in three goals in the space of 15 minutes – his third came just one minute after Alan Shearer had slammed in his 100th Premiership goal for Newcastle to give them some hope. It was a bad day for defenders and goalkeepers, but a great game for strikers and the fans who love to watch them.

United's other league match in November was nowhere near as exciting. Ruud also scored in that one, away to West Ham, but the Reds had to swallow some of their own medicine when Jermain Defoe scored an equaliser just four minutes before the final whistle.

Above: **Diego does it again, this time scoring the winner against Southampton.**

Left: **The old guard. United legend Peter Schmeichel … playing for City!**

High Spot: The fantastic 5–3 win over Newcastle. What a game!
Low Spot: Losing to City for the first time in 13 years.

Man Utd 2–1 Southampton
02-11-2002 (P. Neville 15, Forlan 85)
Man City 3–1 Man Utd
09-11-2002 (Solskjaer 8)
West Ham 1–1 Man Utd
17-11-2002 (van Nistelrooy 38)
Man Utd 5–3 Newcastle Utd
23-11-2002 (Scholes 25, Solskjaer 55, van Nistelrooy 38, 45, 53)

Phil Neville bangs in a rare goal at home to Southampton.

December 2002

United fans didn't know whether to laugh or cry when the fixture computer produced two massive games to start December with. Liverpool away, and then Arsenal at home, separated by just six days. If the Reds lost them both, they could basically kiss goodbye to their chances of winning the championship. On the other hand, if United won both matches, it would mean they were back in business … big time!

Thankfully, that's what happened. United might have struggled earlier in the season against teams like Bolton, Leeds and Manchester City, but against the really big clubs they were on fire. First, Liverpool were put to the sword, with a bit of help from the Anfield goalkeeper Dudek who clumsily allowed a back-header from a team-mate

Top: Forlan can hardly believe his luck after scoring his first at Liverpool.
Below: There's no stopping him now! Forlan fires in number two.

to creep through his hands, arms, legs … everything! Luckily for United, Diego Forlan was waiting on the other side to bury the loose ball into the net. Moments later, it was 2–0 to the Reds, thanks to the same scorer, and a new song was born. "Di-ego, who-oa. Diego, who-oa-a-o. He comes from Uruguay, he made the Scousers cry …" It was an excellent team performance, but one bit of individual brilliance ensured United grabbed the win they fully deserved

– Fabien Barthez made one of the saves of the season to prevent Hamann's long-range rocket from levelling the scores.

Fabien's next feat was to do what other goalkeepers had failed to do in 55 consecutive matches – stop Arsenal from scoring. He did so with the help of a solid back four of Gary Neville at right-back, Mikael Silvestre and Wes Brown as the centre-backs, and John O'Shea on the left. That unit kept Henry, Bergkamp and Pires

Above: **Seba Veron puts a crucial goal past Arsenal keeper Rami Shaaban.**
Right: **Solskjaer heads in the first one of three against West Ham.**

quiet, and then stayed together for the next four games in all competitions, conceding only one goal.

At the other end, it was Juan Sebastian Veron and Paul Scholes who stuffed Arsenal with two high-quality goals. Veron also scored in the next league victory, at home to West Ham – while Beckham and Keane were both injured, the Argentine star clearly enjoyed his new role as the number one midfielder. It was perhaps no coincidence that he was missing when United drew a blank against Blackburn – it was the first league match they had failed to score in since September. Ex-Man City star Flitcroft scored the winning goal for Rovers.

Veron was back on Boxing Day for the game against Middlesbrough, managed by Sir Alex Ferguson's former right-hand man Steve McClaren. Roy Keane also made his long-awaited return, while Beckham came on as sub, but it was all to no avail.

The big stars were perhaps a touch too rusty at the Riverside, and Boro took full advantage to inflict United's heaviest defeat of the season so far.

Facing old friends seemed to be a theme for United during the festive period. After losing to Andy Cole and Dwight Yorke at Blackburn and then Steve McClaren at Middlesbrough, the Reds took on their former captain Steve Bruce at Old Trafford. It was the match that Brucey had been dreaming of since the start of his managerial career, but goals by Forlan and Beckham turned it into a nightmare for him and his Birmingham team in the final league match of 2002.

High Spot: Beating the old enemies Liverpool and Arsenal in back-to-back games.
Low Spot: Losing to old friends like Andy Cole (Blackburn) and Steve McClaren (Middlesbrough).

Liverpool 1–2 Man Utd
01-12-2002 (Forlan 64, 67)
Man Utd 2–0 Arsenal
07-12-2002 (Veron 22, Scholes 73)
Man Utd 3–0 West Ham
14-12-2002 (Solskjaer 15, Veron 17, Schemmel own-goal 61)
Blackburn 1–0 Man Utd
22-12-2002
Middlesbrough 3–1 Man Utd
26-12-2002 (Giggs 60)
Man Utd 2–0 Birmingham City
28-12-2002 (Forlan 37, Beckham 73)

Becks celebrates the second goal against Birmingham.

January 2003

United really turned up the heat on Arsenal in January 2003, winning all three of their league matches in the first month of the new year. Games against Premiership strugglers Sunderland and West Brom might have looked easy on paper but in truth they weren't. In fact, in all of their January league games, the Reds had to claw their way back after conceding the first goal.

On New Year's Day, for example, they were stunned against Sunderland when, after only five minutes, Juan Sebastian Veron headed the ball up and over Rio Ferdinand and into his own net. It was agony for the Argentinian to then

Top: Ruud rifles the equaliser past West Brom keeper Russell Hoult.
Below right: Forlan fires in the winner against Chelsea as Scholes looks on.
Below left: Rio congratulates David on scoring against Sunderland.

look at the scoreboard and see 0–1 for the next 76 minutes until United finally equalised – Seba had fellow midfielder David Beckham to thank for sparing his blushes! If that was tough luck on the Black Cats, then life got even tougher for them in the dying seconds when Scholes struck the second goal to turn what could have been an embarrassing draw into an important 2–1 win.

United were quicker to bounce back in their next league match... much, much quicker. In fact, the West Brom fans were still bouncing up and down in celebration of their opening goal by Koumas when Ruud van Nistelrooy pounced at the other end. With only six minutes on the clock, the score at The Hawthorns was 1–1. Everyone, quite rightly, expected a massive score-line. In the end, only two more goals were added, both to United's tally, by Scholes in the 23rd minute and Solskjaer, ten minutes after half-time. Scholes also scored in United's third and final league game of January. This time, the opponents were from the higher end of the table and they came with a good history of results at Old Trafford. Chelsea beat the Reds 3–0 in Manchester during 2001/02 and they were hoping for a repeat in 2002/03 when Gudjohnsen put

them 1–0 up. But Scholes equalised nine minutes later to leave the game on a knife-edge until the end of normal time when Forlan fired in a tremendous winning goal from Veron's floated pass. Old Trafford erupted with the relief of taking maximum points when two had looked certain to be dropped. And of course, in such a moment of high drama, Diego's shirt just had to come off!

High Spot: Choose from two last-minute winners at home to Sunderland and Chelsea.
Low Spot: Juan Sebastian Veron's embarrassing own goal... two players, together worth £58m, couldn't keep the ball out.

Man Utd 2–1 Sunderland
01-01-2003 (Beckham 81, Scholes 90)
West Brom 1–3 Man Utd
11-01-2003 (Van Nistelrooy 8, Scholes 23, Solskjaer 55)
Man Utd 2–1 Chelsea
18-01-2003 (Scholes 39, Forlan 90)

MANCHESTER UNITED ANNUAL 2004

February 2003

February was a month of two halves. For the first two fixtures, the Reds were in great form. But the next two saw them stumble and lose points to their local rivals.

United started the month by making one of their longest journeys, all the way to the south coast of England. There they encountered an ex-United star in the shape of Southampton boss Gordon Strachan, who played for Sir Alex Ferguson at Aberdeen and then at Old Trafford. Strachan's Saints were having a successful season but any hopes of upsetting his old manager were dashed after just 22 minutes. By then United were 2–0 up thanks to two lightning attacks down the right wing. First, Gary Neville crossed for Ruud to volley in from six yards out. Then Van Nistelrooy set up Giggs who scored at the second attempt.

Van The Man also delivered the goods on United's next road-trip, their first league visit to Birmingham since 1986. On a cold Tuesday night, it was more of a battle than

Top: **Keane keeps the ball away from Bolton's Okocha.**
Below left: **Roy, Gary and Ole help Ruud to celebrate at Southampton.**

a beautiful game, but the Reds were rough enough and tough enough to take all three points, thanks to Ruud's goal on the turn in the second half.

Unfortunately United were less successful in more familiar surroundings. Back at Old Trafford, they dropped points in the Manchester Derby. The Reds made a rampant start, scoring after 18 minutes – Ruud yet again – and dominating the first half. Sadly they couldn't find a second goal, and City came surging back to equalise with Shaun Goater's first touch after coming on as a late substitute. Losing 3–1 to the Blues at Maine Road had been a nightmare, drawing 1–1 at home was not a dream result either.

The break for international action did United few favours as far as the Premiership was concerned. Thirteen days after the Derby draw, the Reds were lucky not to lose to another local team, Bolton.

Sam Allardyce's team took the lead after one hour and they would have built on that lead had Fabien Barthez not made some brilliant saves for United. For all his heroics, Fab could hardly be expected to equalise as well. That important job was left to Ole Gunnar Solskjaer who scored, in typical fashion, in the 90th minute!

Ryan rides a challenge by City's Horlock.

High Spot: Scoring two goals in the space of seven minutes to sink Southampton.
Low Spot: Conceding a goal and dropping two points in the 86th minute against City.

Southampton 0–2 Man Utd
01-02-2003 (Van Nistelrooy 15, Giggs 22)
Birmingham 0–1 Man Utd
04-02-2003 (Van Nistelrooy 56)
Man Utd 1–1 Man City
09-02-2003 (Van Nistelrooy 18)
Bolton 1–1 Man Utd
22-02-2003 (Solskjaer 90)

March 2003

After faltering in February, United's march to the title really started in March. Brushing aside their Worthington Cup woes, the Reds got back to winning ways in the Premiership with a slender but sweet victory in the "battle of the roses" with Leeds. The red rose of Lancashire triumphed against the white of Yorkshire thanks to Mikael Silvestre's first and only goal of the season. With only 11 minutes left and the scores level at 1–1, the French defender stooped to nod in the vital strike.

Only one goal separated the sides in United's next league game, away to Aston Villa. This time the hero was David Beckham; fortunately for Fergie's nerves, he dealt the killer blow nice and early in the twelfth minute of the match, finishing off a good team move with a prod at the far post. Plenty of goal-mouth action followed but both goalkeepers, particularly Fabien Barthez, were on top form.

Barthez kept another clean sheet when Fulham visited Old Trafford, but quite rightly the reports in the Sunday newspapers were all about Ruud van Nistelrooy. The third hat-trick of his United career helped the Reds to regain top spot in the Premiership, at least for 24 hours. Two of the goals were routine – a deflected tap-in during injury time and a penalty just before half-time. But the other was superb, and was immediately heralded as one of the best goals ever scored at Old Trafford. Receiving a pass inside his own half, Ruud raced 60 yards through a maze of bewildered Fulham players before slotting the ball past goalkeeper Mark Taylor. Was it as good a goal as Giggsy's in '99 at Villa Park? Ryan, eat your heart out!

High Spot: Ruud's hat-trick against Fulham, especially for that fantastic goal.
Low Spot: None in the league, only woe in the Worthington Cup (see page 36).

Man Utd 2–1 Leeds Utd
05-03-2003 (Radebe own goal 20, Silvestre 79)
Aston Villa 0–1 Man Utd
15-03-2003 (Beckham 12)
Man Utd 3–0 Fulham
22-03-2003 (Van Nistelrooy 45 pen., 68, 90)

Above: **Ruud roars after his first of three against Fulham.**
Below: **Silvestre celebrates his vital goal versus Leeds.**

April 2003

April showers were scarce as the fine spring weather continued but it rained goals for the Reds. As a result, they would reign supreme when May came around. United netted 17 league goals during April, starting with four against Liverpool. Gerard Houllier's men might have won the Worthington Cup but they were well and truly off the pace in the Premiership, even more so when Ruud van Nistelrooy, Ryan Giggs and Ole Gunnar Solskjaer scored against them at Old Trafford. Ruud's pair were both penalties, the first after he was fouled in the area by Liverpool skipper Sami Hyypia. The Finnish international was sent off after just five minutes!

Seven days later, the live TV audience witnessed another goal-feast. The margin of victory was again four in United's favour, but this time the score was more familiar to tennis lovers than followers of football. The Reds romped to a 6–2 triumph in Newcastle's own backyard, thanks to Ole's

Scholes slams in his first at Newcastle.

equaliser, a sparkling hat-trick by Scholes, a shot on the rebound by Ryan and yet another spot-kick by Ruud. It was game, set and match to United long before Shola Ameobi grabbed a consolation strike for the shell-shocked Magpies. You might recall (from page 9) they lost 5–3 to the Reds earlier in the season!

Big wins against two of their biggest rivals were just what United needed before the biggest game of them all, away to Arsenal. It was felt that the winners of the so-called six-pointer would almost certainly go on to win the title, so the eventual result of 2–2 left everything on a knife-edge. The Reds arguably had a slight advantage at the end; they had

High Spot: Too many to mention; April was an amazing month for Manchester United.
Low Spot: Going from 1–0 up to 2–1 down at Arsenal. Luckily the gloom didn't last long!

Man Utd 4–0 Liverpool
05-04-2003 (Van Nistelrooy 5, 65 pens, Giggs 78, Solskjaer 90)
Newcastle 2–6 Man Utd
12-04-2003 (Solskjaer 32, Scholes 34, 38, 52, Giggs 44, Van Nistelrooy 58 pen.)
Arsenal 2–2 Man Utd
16-04-2003 (Van Nistelrooy 24, Giggs 63)
Man Utd 3–1 Blackburn
19-04-2003 (Van Nistelrooy 20, Scholes 42, 61)
Tottenham 0–2 Man Utd
27-04-2003 (Scholes 68, Van Nistelrooy 90)

looked the better side and were buoyant after coming from behind at Highbury. Not many visiting teams have achieved that but United did, thanks to another goal by the in-form Giggs, scored less than a minute after Thierry Henry had ominously put Arsenal 2–1 up. Race on!

After playing Newcastle, Liverpool and Arsenal, the next two games looked like pieces of cake on paper. But two American goalkeepers, Blackburn's Brad Friedel and Tottenham's Kasey Keller, made the Reds work hard for their eventual victories. Scholes and Van Nistelrooy were the only players to beat the talented shot-stoppers, in both games. A third goalkeeper – United's third-choice Ricardo – made sure of his share in the limelight by giving away and then saving David Dunn's penalty, immediately after coming on as a sub in the Blackburn match. It was a crucial moment as United were only 2–1 up at the time but Ricardo's athletic leap to his left saved the day … and possibly his job!

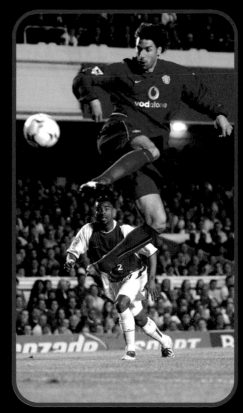

Above: **Ruud attacks the Gunners.**
Below: **Read it and weep, Houllier!**

The Reds savour the sweet taste of revenge against Liverpool.

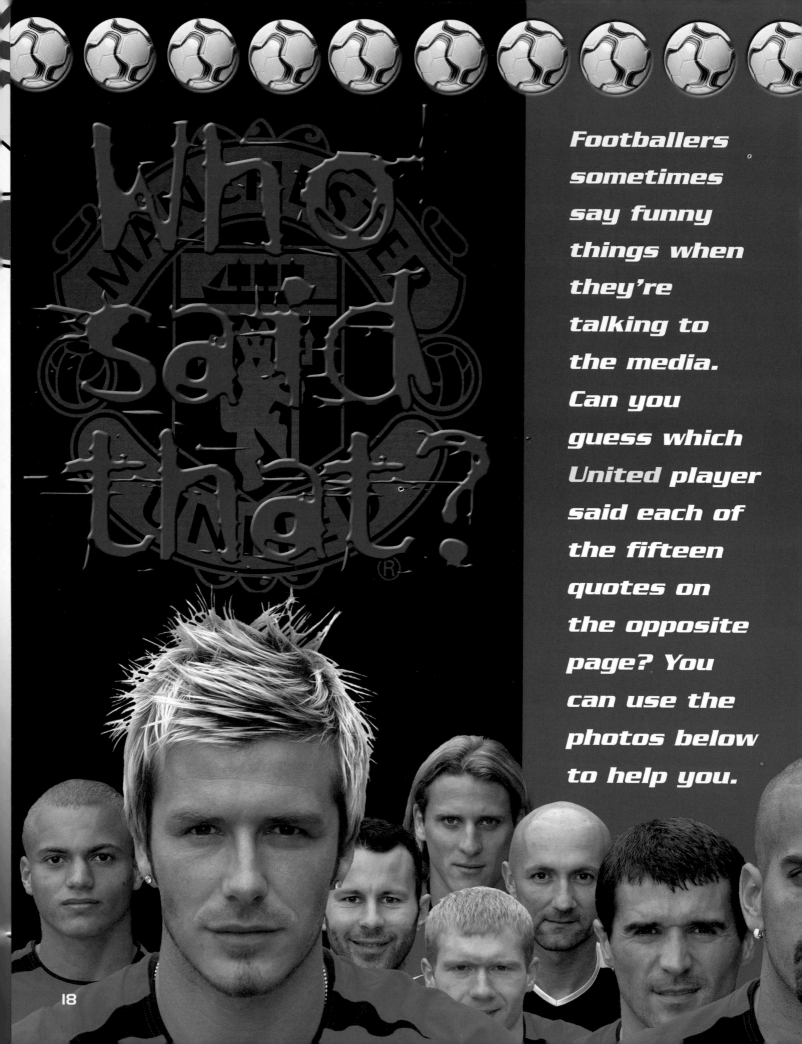

Who Said That?

Footballers sometimes say funny things when they're talking to the media. Can you guess which United player said each of the fifteen quotes on the opposite page? You can use the photos below to help you.

"When Becks wants you to kick the ball he yells 'hit it', which sounds really funny. We're always imitating him, but he doesn't mind, he just laughs."

1

"I was at Manchester City when I was a kid, but they turned me down. I love telling people that!"

2

"I was flicking from channel to channel when we played Basel because I'm a hopeless watcher. I get really nervous. Then, against Liverpool, I couldn't switch the picture on until we were 1-0 up. It's daft really but that's how I am. I jumped off the settee when the second goal went in."

3

"I can be a pain in the backside to play with. People think I'm always having a go at them, giving them stick – but I love all of them. I know they are not listening to me anyway. They're looking at me thinking, 'OK, have your little tantrum and let's get on with it.' "

4

"Criticism is not something I need to dwell on and I don't watch sports programmes anyway. Lately I've been too busy watching the Teletubbies!"

5

"I scored away at Millwall when I was on loan with Bournemouth. It was right in front of their fans – I got a great reception for that!"

6

"If people want to call me the saviour of Manchester United, that's not a problem for me."

7

"Usher is a hero of mine and I'm one of his. He came to the England-Greece game and watched it from my box, then I gave him a couple of England shirts and my boots after the game. I always have his music on."

8

"I've had a bit of a love-hate relationship with the Liverpool fans in the last couple of years."

9

"Unconsciously, I fell in love with the small round sphere with its amusing and capricious rebounds which sometimes play with me."

10

"The Brazilians were South American, and the Ukrainians will be more European."

11

"I've never enjoyed doing interviews. I always run out of the back door of the training ground to avoid the press. I jump into my car and drive off, leaving it to the others."

12

"As a striker, it is not very far from heaven to hell."

13

"It was a good goal and I just didn't know what to do. I ran off thinking, 'I've just scored against Brazil – can someone wake me up here!'"

14

"I had difficulty putting the shirt back on. I ran away to celebrate and then got into a bit of a mess. I was trying to get it back on quickly, but sometimes when you are in a hurry, things tend to get worse."

15

Now turn to page 60 to find out how well you did.

19

Barthez

Full Name: Fabien Barthez
Born: 28 June 1971,
Lavelanet, France
Position: Goalkeeper
Height: 180cm
Weight: 80kg
Nickname: Fab
Transfer Fee: £7.5 million
(from AS Monaco)
Other Previous Clubs:
Toulouse, Olympique Marseille

United's number 1 may be eccentric and slightly shorter than your average keeper, but he's consistently done the business for the Reds …

Goals and Glory

Fabien joined United in May 2000 as a World Cup winner, and within a couple of months he had also won the European Championships with France. Earlier in his career, he lifted the European Cup with Marseille (1993), before moving to Monaco, where he helped to knock United out of the Champions League (1998). The eccentric Frenchman added the Premiership to his medal collection in his first season in England. He continues to enhance his reputation as one of the world's best keepers with some stunning displays between the sticks.

Style and Substance

Fabien isn't tall for a goalkeeper, but he makes up for his lack of stature with an incredibly agile style of play that sees him pull off saves that other goalkeepers would find impossible. He could hardly be more different from his most famous predecessor, Peter Schmeichel – Fab is less inclined to bark orders at his defenders but he's more likely to stray towards the halfway line when the play's at the other end of the pitch.

Fan Chant
(to the tune of "Dirty Old Town")
"Fabien Barthez, Fabien Barthez, Fabien Barthez, Fabien Barthez."

Fergie says:
"The beauty of Fabien Barthez is that he came here with a great record. He's been in World Cup finals, European Championship finals, he won the European Cup with Marseille, and he's got five championship medals. But it's more than just his CV – he's got that wonderful character and personality that we used to have here with Peter Schmeichel. He's a marvellous goalkeeper."

Funny Story
Fabien's first drive to United's training HQ at Carrington ended up with the Frenchman getting hopelessly lost! He took a wrong turning along the way and ended up in Liverpool, of all places! Thankfully he found a kindly Liverpudlian (must have been an Everton fan) who directed him back towards Manchester.

MANCHESTER UNITED ANNUAL 2004

Full name: David Robert Joseph Beckham
Born: 2 May 1975, Leytonstone, London
Position: **Midfielder**
Height: **183cm**
Weight: **76kg**
Nickname: **Becks**
Transfer Fee: **£0** (signed as a trainee)
Previous Clubs: **None**

David is probably the most famous footballer in the world, and also one of the most expensive, following his £25million transfer to Real Madrid…

Goals and Glory

David sprang to prominence when United's kids won the 1992 FA Youth Cup with a team that boasted Becks, Paul Scholes, Gary Neville, Nicky Butt and Ryan Giggs.

David made his first team debut the following season, 1992/93, against Brighton and Hove Albion in the League Cup. However, he then had to wait until April 1995 to make his full league debut, at home to Leeds United. Since then he's won the Premiership, the FA Cup, the European Cup and the Inter-Continental Cup.

David was named England captain by caretaker manager Peter Taylor in November 2000, and he has held onto the armband ever since. His injury-time free-kick against Greece at Old Trafford took England to the 2002 World Cup Finals, where he captained his country in all five games despite having broken a metatarsal bone in his foot in the weeks leading up to the tournament.

Style and Substance

Becks is said to prefer a role in the centre of midfield, but he's undoubtedly more dangerous in his more familiar position wide on the right of midfield. David isn't blessed with as much pace as Ryan Giggs, but his ability to deliver those killer crosses made him a priceless weapon in United's armoury.

David's habit of scoring with direct free-kicks is legendary, so much so that defenders are just as careful not to commit fouls just outside the box as they are inside it! That's not to say he's a one-trick pony, however – some of his best goals have been from open play, including a gem against his new club Real Madrid in 2000 and another in the FA Cup semi-final replay in 1999 against Arsenal (when Giggs scored his famous goal).

Fergie says:

"It's been a pleasure to see David grow and develop into the player he has become. David has been an integral part of all the successes that Manchester United have achieved in the last decade. I would like to wish him and his family every success in the future, and thank him for his service to the club."

Funny Story

The joke was on David when Ali G interviewed Mr and Mrs Beckham in aid of TV charity event Comic Relief. *"Is your boy starting to string together sentences now?"* Ali asked Victoria. *"Yes, he's doing very well,"* she replied, falling into the trap. *"And what about Brooklyn?"* followed up Ali, to great laughter from the audience!

Goodbye and good luck, David, and thanks for the memories!

Beckham

United by

How well do you know your United numbers? Try out our quiz to see if you're up to scratch on the facts and figures of your favourite team.

We've set 28 teasers for you to answer. Why not challenge a friend to see who can answers the most questions? Good luck!

How many goals did Ruud score in his first season?

Tall, short, old, young

 Laurent Blanc was the oldest player to make a first team appearance in 2002/03. How old was he?
(a) 37 (b) 35 (c) 39

 And how old was Darren Fletcher – the youngest to make an appearance?
(a)17 (b) 18 (c) 19

3 How tall is John O'Shea – the tallest member of the first team squad?
(a) 6´0˝ (b) 6´3˝ (c) 6´7˝

numbers

 4 And how tall is the shortest player – Paul Scholes?
(a) 5'7" (b) 5'5" (c) 5'9"

 5 How old was Billy Meredith when he scored his final United goal?
(a) 50 years, 92 days
(b) 48 years, 201 days
(c) 42 years, 190 days

 6 Who is the youngest player to have scored for the Reds, at the age of 17 years and 7 days?
(a) Norman Whiteside
(b) David Beckham
(c) Paul Scholes

 7 What is the weight of the joint heaviest players at Old Trafford, Roy Carroll and Rio Ferdinand?
(a) 12st 7lb (b) 14st 3lb
(c) 13st 12lb

Goals and glory

 1 How many league goals did club record-holder Sir Bobby Charlton score for United?
(a) 199 (b) 299 (c) 399

 2 Who has made the most league appearances for United in club history, with a total of 606?
(a) George Best (b) Denis Irwin
(c) Sir Bobby Charlton

 3 How many goals did Ruud van Nistelrooy score in his first season at Old Trafford in all competitions (including the Charity Shield)?
(a) 36 (b) 27 (c) 45

 4 Who did United beat 9–0 in March 1995 – still a Premiership record?
(a) West Ham (b) Barnsley
(c) Ipswich Town

 5 How long did it take Ryan Giggs to score United's fastest-ever goal, against Southampton in November 1995?
(a) 1 minute 2 seconds
(b) 51 seconds (c) 15 seconds

 6 Peter Schmeichel holds the league record for consecutive clean sheets at home. For how many games did he keep the ball out of the net?
(a) 4 (b) 12 (c) 17

 7 How many Premiership, FA Cup, League Cup, European Cup and Cup Winners' Cup medals did Denis Irwin win with United to make him the most successful player in Reds history?
(a)12 (b)13 (c)14

History and heritage

 1 In which year were United founded, under the name Newton Heath?
(a)1848 (b) 1878 (c) 1902

 2 What was the score in United's first home match in the European Cup, against Anderlecht?
(a) 1–0 (b) 5–0 (c) 10–0

 3 What is the biggest crowd United have ever played in front of, against Real Madrid in 1956?
(a) 135,000 (b) 150,000
(c) 75,000

4 How many full-time managers have United had in their history?
(a) 7 (b) 15 (c) 12

5 How many times have the Reds been League Champions?
(a) 7 (b) 21 (c) 15

 6 How many goals did George Best score against Northampton Town in the 1970 FA Cup run?
(a) 4 (b) 5 (c) 6

 7 How many hat-tricks did Denis Law score for the Reds?
(a) 14 (b) 12 (c) 10

Mixed bag

 1 How many Top Ten hits have United had?
(a) 2 (b) 3 (c) 4

 2 How many players in the 2002/03 squad were from overseas?
(a) 9 (b) 10 (c) 11

 3 For how many years was Bryan Robson club captain, making him the longest serving Reds skipper?
(a) 10 (b) 12 (c) 14

 4 How many clubs did Laurent Blanc play for before joining United?
(a) 3 (b) 6 (c) 8

 5 For how many games did United go unbeaten between December 1998 and October 1999?
(a) 33 (b) 45 (c) 57

 6 What is the record transfer fee that United have received for a player? (For Jaap Stam in 2001.)
(a) £7 million (b) £16 million
(c) £20.1 million

 7 How many goals did Blackburn score to cause United's heaviest league defeat in 1926?
(a) 3 (b) 7 (c) 6

Now turn to page 60 to see how well you did.

Ferdinand, For

D-F

What do an English defender, a South African midfielder and a Uruguayan striker all have in common? They're all f-f-f-featured on this page, that's what!

Full Name: **Rio Ferdinand**
Born: **7 November 1978, Peckham, London**
Position: **Defender**
Height: **188cm**
Weight: **77kg**
Transfer Fee: **£30 million**
(from Leeds United)
Other Previous Clubs:
West Ham United

Rio became the most expensive defender in the world when he joined the Reds from Leeds United after the 2002 World Cup. It was in Japan and South Korea that Rio really made his mark, although Sir Alex had tried to buy him before the tournament – and had to watch in horror as his transfer value rose with every superb performance for England. The West Ham graduate went on holiday to Las Vegas with Wes Brown after England's elimination, and lo and behold he signed for United on his return. Remarkably cool under pressure and superb at playing the ball out of defence, Rio has been a fantastic addition to the United backline, where he has formed impressive partnerships with both Wes and Mikael Silvestre. Rio showed his dancing skills after scoring against Denmark at the World Cup, but was slightly out of step when he accidentally slapped referee Steve Bennett in the face while celebrating Phil Neville's goal against West Ham! David Beckham is less than complimentary about Rio's moves, however, saying, *"He's got no rhythm!"*

Fan Chant
(to the tune of *"Hi Ho,Hi,Ho"*)
"Rio,Rio, he is a Red you know. He met El Tel and said farewell, Rio, Rio, Rio, Rio."

Fun Fact
Rio wore a bright white suit on the day he joined United, prompting comparisons with actor John Travolta from 1970s disco movie *Saturday Night Fever*!

Full Name: **Diego Forlan**
Born: **19 May 1979, Montevideo, Uruguay**
Position: **Forward**
Height: **172cm**
Weight: **75kg**
Transfer Fee: **£7.8 million**
(from Independiente, Argentina)
Other Previous Clubs: **None**

Fact file

an and Fortune

Diego signed for United in January 2002, despite Steve McClaren's efforts to take him further north to Middlesbrough. Even when Forlan flew into London's Gatwick, the media couldn't work out if his final stop would be Old Trafford or the Riverside!

The Uruguayan striker received lots of stick from the newspapers when he failed to score in his first 34 appearances, but that was very unfair as he was often only coming on for a few minutes as a substitute. Forlan finally found the net from the penalty spot against Maccabi Haifa, and then scored his first goal from open play against Aston Villa. From then on there was no stopping him, and he netted against Southampton, Burnley, Chelsea (in both the Premiership and the Worthington Cup) and Birmingham City in the following months. But it was his two goals against Liverpool in the 2–1 win at Anfield that made him a firm favourite with the fans.

Diego's hard work on and off the ball while on the pitch and his cheery manner off the pitch have made him hugely popular in the stands and among his team-mates and the staff at the training ground. Middlesbrough's loss is definitely United's gain!

Fan Chant
(to the tune of *"Volare"*)

"Diego, oh oh oh. Diego, oh oh oh oh. He came from Uruguay, he made the Scousers cry!"

Fun Fact
Diego used to play a lot of tennis when he was younger, and had to decide at the age of 14 whether to become a tennis pro or a footballer. Good choice, Diego!

Full Name: Quinton Fortune
Born: 21 May 1977, Cape Town, South Africa
Position: Midfielder
Height: 175cm
Weight: 75kg
Transfer Fee: £1.5 million
(from Atletico Madrid)
Other Previous Clubs: Mallorca

Quinton Fortune made the step up from squad player to first team regular in November 2002, starting five matches in a row and impressing everyone who saw him with his skill, pace and work rate. United won four and drew one of Quinny's quintet of games.

It came as a huge shock and disappointment when it was announced that the South African midfielder had broken his leg in the fifth game of that run – the 2–1 win against Liverpool. In fact, it wasn't announced until a week after that match as Quinton had trained all week despite his injury! Such bad luck was ironic for a player whose surname is Fortune. Three months in the gym saw him beef up – leading to new nicknames of *"The Strongest Man in the World"* and *"Tyson"*, and he made his return to the first team in the 2–1 victory over Leeds at Old Trafford.

Quinton joined the United international army at the 2002 World Cup, scoring a penalty against Paraguay and celebrating like a madman. *"I just couldn't believe I'd scored in the World Cup,"* he said by way of an excuse!

Fun Fact
Quinton Fortune first tried his luck in England with Tottenham Hotspur. He trained with Spurs but couldn't play for them because he couldn't get a work permit.

Fan's Guide to

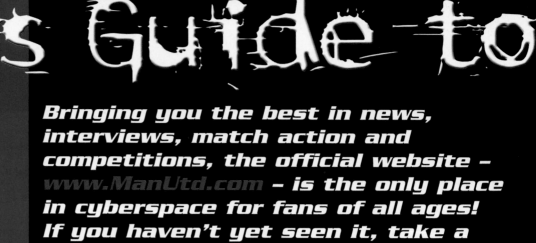

Bringing you the best in news, interviews, match action and competitions, the official website – www.ManUtd.com – is the only place in cyberspace for fans of all ages! If you haven't yet seen it, take a look at what you've been missing.

News and Interviews

From an office in the heart of Old Trafford, a dedicated team of website journalists publishes up-to-the-minute news about Manchester United. You might read transfer rumours elsewhere, but ManUtd.com is always the first website to announce when a new player has actually signed for the club. You can also read exclusive player interviews. Sometimes the player answers questions sent in by the fans! Why not send your question by e-mail when you next log on?

Live Match Coverage

Weekends and weeknights are when ManUtd.com really comes alive. Match Tracker TM – the website's live text commentary service – is updated several times per minute during every game, home or away, with details of goals, corners and more as soon as they happen. Listen to the live radio commentary too, and you'll feel like you're at the match! You can also see live photos during certain games, and even get goal alerts sent to your mobile phone. You can't miss a kick!

Fan Fun

Fans are the most important part of any club, and ManUtd.com makes sure that United fans can have their say on the website. Firstly, there's a live 24-hour chat room where you can discuss recent games and the latest gossip. The FanTalk pages on ManUtd.com are where fan e-mails are published after every match, whatever the result! There's also a new poll on the site every day – voting is easy, just click!

Virtual Tour

Can't get to Old Trafford? Don't worry, you can still have a look around the famous stadium thanks to ManUtd.com's fantastic Virtual Tour. Special cameras give you panoramic views both inside and outside the ground, including superb shots of where the manager stands during the game and the dressing room where the Reds get ready!

ManUtd.com

MU.tv

If you missed the last game, then MU.tv is the ideal service for you! ManUtd.com's online video library contains goal clips and other highlights from every Premier League match that the Reds have played since 1992. There are also plenty of news and interviews for you to watch and enjoy, including some specially recorded conversations with David Beckham and the top man at Old Trafford, Peter Kenyon!

History

The heritage of Manchester United is hugely impressive, and is rightly celebrated on ManUtd.com. You can find profiles of every player who's made at least one first team appearance for the club, details of every manager, and a record of every result since the 1890s!

Shopping

Looking for a special present for the United fan in your family? ManUtd.com's online store stocks everything you'd find in the souvenir shop at Old Trafford – and you can buy it without leaving the comfort of your own home or office!

The Oddkinsons

ManUtd.com is also home to a family of United-loving cartoon characters – The Oddkinsons. The animated adventures of Terence, Colin, Mum, Dad, Uncle Dave and the rest are funny and free to watch. Popular episodes in their first season poked fun at United's arch-rivals from Liverpool and of course, the blue half of Manchester.

MU Now

Got a mobile? Then why not sign up to MU Now, the service that allows you to

download United ringtones and logos, vote on key issues and receive the latest news and match information … including goal alerts!

Competitions

United fans have won holidays, mobile phones, books, videos, CDs and of course match tickets on ManUtd.com. So what are you waiting for? Try your luck today!

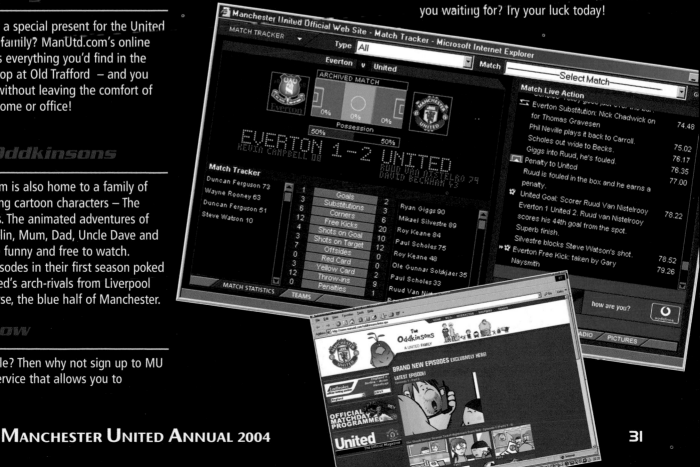

REDS IN EUROPE

For the third time in four seasons since winning the UEFA Champions League, United bowed out of Europe at the quarter-final stage in 2002/03. And it had all started so promisingly ...

Veron fires a shot past Juventus defender Paolo Montero.

of form in the Champions League, winning their first four matches in a row to reach the second group stage in record time. Ruud netted against Maccabi Haifa and Bayer Leverkusen as his quest for the record number of Champions League goals in a season took flight.

The manager could even afford to send out a young squad – featuring the likes of Mads Timm, Daniel Nardiello and Kieran Richardson – to the away match against Maccabi. The juniors lost 3–0 but the experience will serve them well in years to come. United ensured top spot in Group F – and with it a favourable draw in the next phase – with a 2–0 win over Leverkusen at Old Trafford. Revenge!

Qualifying

After finishing third in the Premiership, United had to qualify for the Champions League – a tournament they'd won just four seasons earlier. Their opponents in the qualifying round were an unpronounceable team from Hungary, Zalaegerszeg.

Despite a shock 1–0 defeat in the away leg, the Reds recorded a 5–1 aggregate win after cruising the return leg at Old Trafford. Ruud van Nistelrooy netted his first two goals in what would turn out to be a record-breaking season for him. Beckham, Scholes and Solskjaer also scored.

First Group Stage

Having overcome the commentator's nightmare team, United were drawn against Maccabi Haifa of Israel, Olympiakos of Greece and Germany's Bayer Leverkusen – the side that knocked Sir Alex out of the competition at the semi-final stage in 2001/02.

Although things were not going to plan in the Premiership, Becks and the boys hit a rich vein

Second Group Stage

United were drawn against more "old friends" in the next UEFA mini-league, with Juventus and Deportivo la Coruna joining Liverpool's conquerors Basel in the group of four teams who would fight it out to reach the quarter-finals. The Reds had had many memorable tussles with Juve over the past few seasons – most notably the semi-final second leg in Turin during the Treble season. Deportivo, meanwhile, would be facing United for the fifth and sixth times in the space of eighteen months.

The remarkable run of form continued in the second phase, as Basel and Deportivo were despatched 3–1 and 2–0 respectively before the winter break. Four of the five goals were scored by van Nistelrooy. After the two-month gap, the Reds won both parts of a double-header against Juve, 2–1 at home, with Wes joining Ruud on the scoresheet, and 3–0 in a fantastic match at the Stadio Delle Alpi as Ryan Giggs scored twice to add to a goal from – yes, you guessed it – Ruud!

That result meant that the last two games were of no real consequence for the Reds, as their place at the top of Group D was impossible to lose. Gary Neville scored a blinding left-footed goal against Basel in a 1–1 draw at Old Trafford, while the kids – Mark Lynch, Lee Roche, Danny Pugh and Darren Fletcher – started in a 2–0 away defeat to Deportivo.

The Reds were safely through to the Champions League quarter-finals for a record seventh season in succession, but the draw would pit them against some of the best players on the planet.

Quarter-finals

With the 2002/03 Champions League Final being held at Old Trafford, every United fan wanted the Reds to meet defending champions Real Madrid in the match on May 28. Instead, the draw forced Fergie's men to face Ronaldo, Raul, Zidane, Figo and co in the quarter-final.

A stunning show in the first half of the first leg in the Bernabeu saw Real, arguably the best team in the world, go 2–0 up. Raul then added a third goal shortly after half-time. A lifeline goal from Ruud van Nistelrooy – his eleventh in the Champions League in 2002/03, which beat Alessandro del Piero's previous record – gave the Reds hope for the second leg, where a 2–0 win would be enough to put them through to the semi-finals again.

It wasn't to be, though. A hat-trick from Ronaldo – who was clapped off the pitch by all 67,000 fans in the stadium – and two goals from substitute David Beckham contributed to a fantastic match. United won 4–3 on the night, but it wasn't enough and Madrid went through 6–5 on aggregate after two of the most amazing European games ever seen.

Ruud's goal in that match gave him a total of twelve goals in the 2002/03 Champions League. He also scored two in qualifying matches but UEFA don't count them in their record books. The Euro campaign may have ended in disappointment, but thanks to Ruud, United showed they could live with the best in the world. Roll on 2003/04!

Ruud's record

Ruud van Nistelrooy scored 12 goals in the 2002/03 UEFA Champions League – setting a new record for the competition. Here's the full list:

18/09/02 v **Maccabi Haifa** (1)
24/09/02 v **Bayer Leverkusen** (2)
13/11/02 v **Bayer Leverkusen** (1)
26/11/02 v **FC Basel** (2)
11/12/02 v **Deportivo la Coruna** (2)
19/02/03 v **Juventus** (1)
25/02/03 v **Juventus** (1)
08/04/03 v **Real Madrid** (1)
23/04/03 v **Real Madrid** (1)

* Ruud also scored two against Zalaegerszeg on 27/08/02, but UEFA don't include goals scored in the qualifying rounds.

Ruud pops one in against Real.

The Reds and Real Madrid line up before kick-off at the Bernabeu Stadium.

Giggs

Full Name: **Ryan Giggs**
Born: **29 November 1973, Cardiff**
Position: **Winger**
Height: **180cm**
Weight: **70kg**
Transfer Fee: **£0**
(signed as trainee)
Previous Clubs: **None**

Ryan Giggs is well into his second decade as a fixture in United's first team, and is still thrilling the fans who have followed his incredible career from the word go …

Goals and Glory

Ryan Giggs is on course to become the most decorated player in United history. He has collected a remarkable set of medals in the League, FA Cup, League Cup, Inter-Continental Cup and the European Cup. His first taste of team success came in 1992 when he led the Reds to FA Youth Cup glory.

Giggsy also won an impressive haul of individual awards in the early part of his career. He was named PFA Young Player of the Year in 1992 and 1993, making him the first man ever to win it twice. He's also the youngest player to have turned out for Wales – he did so at the age of 17 years and 321 days. He also won the Barclays Bank Young Eagle of the Year in 1992, to add to two Jimmy Murphy Young Player of the Year awards in 1991 and 1992. Ryan has since fulfilled all that potential, and has become one of the greatest home-grown players in United history.

Style and Substance

Ryan Giggs' emergence at Old Trafford breathed new life into the club. The sight of the dashing young winger taking on and beating more established and experienced players signalled a new dawn for Manchester United, and just two years after his debut the Reds were celebrating their first League Championship for 26 years.

Giggsy's pace was the thing that marked him out from the crowd from an early age, but as he's matured he's added more tricks to his game and his crossing has improved to make him the complete winger. People used to say that George Best would leave his opponents with "twisted blood!" Ryan has a similar effect on modern-day defenders … just ask the Arsenal players who tried to stop him scoring that sublime goal in the 1999 FA Cup semi-final replay! Marking him is still hard work!

Fan Chant
(To the tune of *"Robin Hood"*)
"Ryan Giggs, Ryan Giggs, running down the wing. Ryan Giggs, Ryan Giggs, can do anything. Feared by the Blues, loved by the Reds. Ryan Giggs, Ryan Giggs, Ryan Giggs."

Fergie says:
"I knew we had an outstanding talent when we gave him his debut and he's been a special player for the last ten years. When he plays at the level he is capable of there are few who can touch him in the world. He's a constant worry to defences and despite being a fantastic individual talent, he also works hard for the team."

Keane

G-K

Full name:
Roy Maurice Keane
Born: 10 August 1971,
Cork, Ireland,
Position: **Midfield**
Height: **180cm**
Weight: **74kg**
Transfer Fee: **£3.75 million**
(from Nottingham Forest)
Other Previous Clubs: **Cobh Ramblers**

United's skipper is the team's heartbeat, the man that the players look to for inspiration and motivation. He's got plenty of both to spare …

Goals and Glory

Since joining Manchester United in July 1993, Roy Keane has won countless trophies. And although the Reds might have won the European Cup Final without him in 1999, they might not have been in it had it not been for captain Keano's superhuman display in the semi-final. What made his performance all the more admirable was the fact that Keano knew he would miss the final after being booked during the semi against Juve.

Many United fans pick out Roy as their favourite because of his never-say-die attitude and his willingness to put his body on the line for his team. Football journalists and his fellow professionals named him Player of the Year in 1999/2000.

Roy played for the Republic of Ireland in the 1994 World Cup Finals, helping them to reach the last sixteen. He has since retired from the international scene for medical reasons, leaving him free to concentrate on his United career.

Style and Substance

Roy is often described as Sir Alex Ferguson's representative out on the pitch, because of the way he'll cajole and harangue his team-mates into improving their performances.

In 2002/03, Roy admitted he'd tried to change his style of play. *"In the past I've tried to do everything, from clearing a shot off the line one minute to trying to score up the other end the next. When I was out injured, I thought to myself, 'My team-mates are pretty talented, why don't I let them do the running for me?' So that's what I'm trying to do – less of the headless chicken routine, I'm using my head more."*

Fan Chant

"Keano! There's only one Keano! There's only one Keano! There's only one Keano!"

Fergie says:

"If I was going to put Roy Keane out there to represent Manchester United on a one to one, we'd win the Derby, the Grand National, the Boat Race and anything else. Roy is an unbelievable player whose leadership, passion and drive epitomise the best qualities of Manchester United. I think he is the best player I've had."

Funny Story

Roy watched Ireland play in the 1990 World Cup in a pub back home in Cork, where the landlord had promised to give out free pints of beer for every goal Ireland scored. Their last-sixteen match against Romania went to penalties, with David O'Leary scoring the final spot-kick to make the score 5–4. *"They gave us pints for all the penalties, too!"* said Roy a few years later.

The Reds may not have won either of the domestic cups in the 2002/03 season, but they still provided us with plenty of memorable moments on the roads to Cardiff ...

The Worthington Cup

United surprised and delighted many people with their run in the Worthington Cup in 2002/03 after several years of using the competition to try out young players. This time, Sir Alex Ferguson felt he had to pick a much stronger side, especially when the Reds had to play in front of their home fans in several rounds. The end result was that United reached the final for the first time since 1994.

Round Three: 5 November 2002
United 2 Leicester City 0

The road to Cardiff started at home, with the visit of First Division Leicester City to Old Trafford on Bonfire Night. The fireworks came courtesy of David Beckham and Kieran Richardson, who scored his first senior goal for the club – a brave diving header – to help see off the Foxes.

Round Four: 3 December 2002
Burnley 0 United 2

United were drawn away to north-west neighbours Burnley in the last sixteen, and goals from Diego Forlan – who'd scored two against Liverpool just two days earlier – and Ole Gunnar Solskjaer clinched a place in the quarter-finals.

Round Five: 17 December 2002
United 1 Chelsea 0

The last eight pitted Fergie's men against Premiership opposition for the first time in the cup run – high-flying Chelsea. "I knew they'd put a strong team out, and with them coming back to Old Trafford in the league in four weeks I didn't want them to have any psychological advantage. I had to go for it," said Sir Alex. His strong team selection paid off as the Reds beat the Blues 1–0 with another late goal from Diego.

Forlan celebrates against Chelsea.

Semi-Final First Leg: 7 January 2003
United 1 Blackburn 1

Semi-Final Second Leg: 22 January 2003
Blackburn 1 United 3

The semi-final against the cup-holders Blackburn was left on a knife-edge when the rivals drew 1–1 in the first leg at Old Trafford. But any worries that United might miss out on Cardiff were dispelled with a ruthless perfomance at Ewood Park. Paul Scholes followed up his first-leg goal with another important strike and Ruud van Nistelrooy bagged the other two. Fergie's men were in the final!

Final: 2 March 2003
Liverpool 2 United 0

Any match against Liverpool is greatly anticipated, but with the first trophy of the season at stake, the Worthington Cup Final was a tense affair for all concerned.

United were slow out of the blocks in the first half. Their supporters saw good chances come and go, but it was the Liverpool fans who really raised the roof when Steven Gerrard made it 1–0 with a shot that deflected off unlucky David Beckham.

United played much better in the second half, but Liverpool goalkeeper Jerzy Dudek was equal to everything that Ruud and the lads could throw at him – making up for his crucial mistake in the league game at Anfield in December. With time running out, a misplaced chest-down from Mikael Silvestre was pounced on by Dietmar Hamann, who set up England striker Michael Owen to score Liverpool's killer second goal.

The United fans went home disappointed, but vowing to return to Cardiff one day!

The FA Cup

United have won the FA Cup a record ten times in their history, and they were determined to make it eleven after three years of missing out. The Reds didn't defend their trophy in 1999/2000 – instead

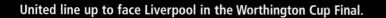

United line up to face Liverpool in the Worthington Cup Final.

they went to Brazil – and they were knocked out in the following two seasons by West Ham and Middlesbrough.

Third Round: 4 January 2003
United 4 Portsmouth 1

Sir Alex was drawn against his old friend Harry Redknapp when United joined the tournament in its third round. Redknapp's Portsmouth were then at the top of Division One, with experienced players like Paul Merson and Shaka Hislop in their team, but they couldn't handle United's firepower. Ruud van Nistelrooy netted twice from the penalty spot, and was joined on the scoresheet by Beckham and Scholes.

Fourth Round: 26 January 2003
United 6 West Ham 0

Memories of United's painful defeat in 2000 came flooding back when they were pulled out of the hat against West Ham in 2003. Thankfully there was to be no repeat this time, as the rampant Reds stormed home 6–0 with goals from Ryan Giggs (2),

Ruud (2), Ole Gunnar Solskjaer and Phil Neville. Yes, Phil Neville!

Fifth Round: 15 February 2003
United 0 Arsenal 2

United old-boys Bryan Robson and Gary Pallister made the draw that pitted the great rivals against each other. The Reds had already beaten Arsenal at Old Trafford earlier in the season, but this had no bearing on the cup tie. The Gunners won 2–0 to end United's FA Cup dream … for another year!

Van The Man in action against Portsmouth.

the Nevilles

L–O

Full-backs are football's unsung heroes. Let's pay tribute to three *United* **defenders who rarely make the headlines ...**

Full Name: **Gary Neville**
Born: **18 February 1975, Bury**
Position: **Defender**
Height **180cm**
Weight: **79kg**
Transfer Fee: **£0** (signed as trainee)
Previous Clubs: **None**

Gary Neville is one of the most experienced defenders in the modern game, having made more appearances in the UEFA Champions League than any other player. He's also closing in on his fifth century of appearances for United in all competitions, and as if that's not enough, he's also a regular member of the England squad!

Gary's right-wing partnership with David Beckham has benefited both club and country over the years. Becks does most of the attacking, of course, but Gaz has been known to send over some dangerous crosses after overlapping the England captain. The elder Neville has even scored a handful of goals – literally, you can count them on one hand! The fourth goal of his career came against Basel in the 2002/03 Champions League when he was captaining the side in Keane's absence. *"I'd still love to score a big goal in a big game,"* said Gary. *"I couldn't really get carried away with the Basel goal, but I did have a smile to myself while running back afterwards!"*

Fan Chant
(tune *"London Bridge is falling down"*)
"Gary Neville is a Red, is a Red, is a Red. Gary Neville is a Red. He hates Scousers!"

Fun Fact
Gary is the chief organiser in the dressing room. Whenever the lads go off horse racing, golfing, go-karting or paint-balling, Gary's the one who sorts it all out!

Full Name: **Philip Neville**
Born: **21 January 1977, Bury**
Position: **Defender/Midfielder**
Height: **180cm**
Weight: **75kg**
Transfer Fee: **£0** (signed as trainee)
Previous Clubs: **None**

Every United fan should know about the 1992 FA Youth Cup winning team that featured Gary Neville, Beckham, Butt, Giggs and Scholes, but it's sometimes forgotten that Phil Neville played in the 1995 side that also won the competition.

Mind you, Phil's used to being overlooked and under-praised, but that all changed in December 2002 when United beat Arsenal 2–0 at Old Trafford. With Roy Keane and Nicky Butt out injured, it fell to Phil to become the midfield enforcer. It was

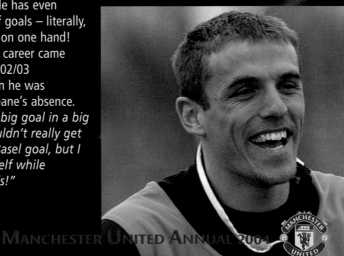

Fact File

38

and O'Shea

no easy task against Patrick Vieira but Phil took charge, winning tackle after tackle.

Having played most of his career at full-back, Phil discovered that he was equally at home in central midfield, and he also made a bid to start in attack with a beautifully taken goal against West Ham in the 6–0 FA Cup win. His modest celebration made out that he'd scored by accident, but he knew exactly what he was doing when he chipped the ball over David James.

Phil's wife, Julie, gave birth to their first child – a son named Harvey – in 2002, so fingers crossed there could be another Neville in the United team in the future!

Fun Fact
David Beckham has known Phil and his brother Gary for years, and knows how talkative they can be, especially when they're together. *"I sit between Phil and Gary at dinner sometimes, and I need to go for a lie down afterwards!"* says David.

Full Name: **John O'Shea**
Born: **30 April 1981, Waterford, Ireland**
Position: **Defender**
Height: **191cm**
Weight: **75kg**
Transfer Fee: **£0** (signed as trainee)
Previous Clubs: **None**

John O'Shea supported Liverpool when he was growing up in Ireland, but thankfully he saw the error of his ways after signing for United in August 1998. Several years later, he emerged as one of the most exciting talents ever to be produced by the United youth system. Hard luck, Liverpool!

John broke into the Reserves as a centre-back, but he has since proved his versatility by playing for the first team at right-back, left-back and in central defence and midfield for the first team. Wonder when he'll play in attack or in goal?

The giant but graceful Irishman is at his most thrilling when breaking out of defence at full-back and scorching down the wing on a jinking run, nut-megging the defenders he leaves in his wake, before putting in a pinpoint cross. He even performed a text-book move called the Cruyff Turn in one match against Leeds!

Perhaps the only blot on John's copybook was the mistake he made on his debut for the Republic of Ireland. He came on as a sub in the 84th minute and immediately gave away a penalty in the 2–2 draw with Croatia! Still, all great players make mistakes now and then, and John definitely has the makings of a great player!

Fan Chant
(tune *"Yesterday"* by The Beatles)
"John O'Shea, oh I believe in John O'Shea."

Fun Fact
Roy Keane has questioned whether Sheasy is really Irish! *"He's too sensible to be Irish,"* laughs Roy. *"He hasn't got that daftness that the rest of us have!"*

"I sit between Phil and Gary at dinner sometimes, and I need to go for a lie down afterwards!"

DAVID BECKHAM

L-O

Fact File

It's little wonder that **Manchester United** have been so successful during the past ten years. You only have to look at this training session to see how ultra-competitive they are. Nobody is more determined to win than the manager himself, Sir Alex Ferguson!

"OK lads, let's finish the training session with a match. Oranges versus Lemons, first goal wins."

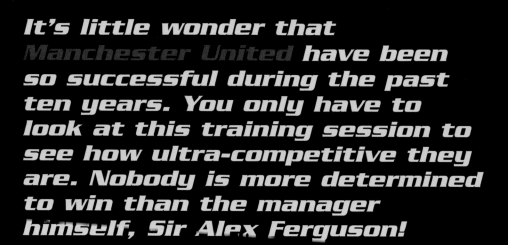

1

Veron: "Hurrah! No more bunny-hops and star-jumps. Time for some proper football at last!"
Forlan: "One thousand and four, one thousand and five … hang on, I've nearly equalled the Uruguayan record."

2

Sir Alex: "Carlos, I want you to referee. I'm going to play … for whichever team looks like winning."
Carlos: "No problem, Boss. Just sneak on when nobody's looking."

3

Sir Alex: "And I want you, Dr Mike, and you, Albert, to be the linesmen. Don't forget, I'm never offside."
Stone and Morgan (together): "Yes, Boss. That's right, Boss. Flag stays down, Boss."

5

Gary Neville: "You can't win five–nil, Mikael. It's first goal wins, you lemon! Besides we're bound to win with the brilliant me and Rio in defence, plus D-I-E-G-O in attack."

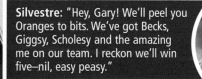

Silvestre: "Hey, Gary! We'll peel you Oranges to bits. We've got Becks, Giggsy, Scholesy and the amazing me on our team. I reckon we'll win five–nil, easy peasy."

4

Oranges a

6

Carlos (blows whistle): "OK, gentlemen, off you go. And remember … first goal wins!"
Ferdinand: "Right Kieran, John … let's get the ball and show those lemons how it's done."

7

Ferdinand: "Got it. Here, Diego, over to you, pal. But if you score, keep your bib on!"

8

Forlan: "Gracias, Rio. Nice pass … for a defender. Hey, Gary, this is for you …"

9

Nardiello: "Not so fast, Mr Forlan! I'll take that, thank you very much. Here, Scholesy, your ball …"

10

11

Scholes: "Great interception, Dan. And what a superb swivel pass. Right, it's time for one of my famous probing passes. Straight to … The Boss!"

12

Sir Alex: "And Ferguson, the brilliant striker from Glasgow, fires home the golden goal. Yes! One–nil! Scotland have won the World Cup!"

13

Carlos: "That's it, time's up. Bad luck, Oranges, the Lemons have won one–nil. Mr Ferguson was the man of the match, no question."

14

Forlan: "No way, Jose! Mr Ferguson cheated. That's not fair!"

15

Sir Alex: "Sorry, Diego, but I think you'll find I was miles onside. Just ask my totally unbiased linesmen. It just goes to show, I'm still the greatest centre-forward in the world. Isn't that right, David?"

16

Beckham (sighs): "Yes, Boss. Of course, Boss."

"Never mind the golden goal, reader. The golden rule is – the Boss is always right!"

Crysta

Fancy yourse

Man U are the best

T his is your chance to impress your fellow United fans by making ten bold predictions for the 2003/04 season. You could even photocopy the page so that your family and friends can challenge you.

Premiership Champions		
2003/04		
2002/03		Manchester United
2001/02		Manchester United
2000/01		Manchester United
1999/00		Manchester United
1998/99		Arsenal

FA Cup Winners		
2003/04		
2002/03		Arsenal
2001/02		Arsenal
2000/01		Liverpool
1999/00		Chelsea
1998/99		Manchester United

League Cup Winners		
2003/04		*Middlesborough*
2002/03		Liverpool
2001/02		Blackburn Rovers
2000/01		Liverpool
1999/00		Leicester City
1998/99		Tottenham Hotspur

UEFA Champions League		
2003/04		
2002/03		AC Milan *(Italy)*
2001/02		Real Madrid *(Spain)*
2000/01		Bayern Munich *(Germany)*
1999/00		Real Madrid *(Spain)*
1998/99		Manchester United *(England)*

UEFA Cup Winners		
2003/04		
2002/03		FC Porto *(Portugal)*
2001/02		Feyenoord *(Netherlands)*
2000/01		Liverpool *(England)*
1999/00		Galatasaray *(Turkey)*
1998/99		Parma *(Italy)*

al Ball

f as a football clairvoyant?

European Championships

2004	
2000	France
1996	Germany
1992	Denmark
1988	Netherlands
1984	France

Premiership Top Scorer

2003/04	
2002/03	Ruud van Nistelrooy *(Man Utd)* **25**
2001/02	Alan Shearer *(Newcastle)* **24**
2000/01	Jimmy Floyd Hasselbaink *(Chelsea)* **18**
1999/00	Kevin Phillips *(Sunderland)* **30**
1998/99	Jimmy Floyd Hasselbaink *(Chelsea)* **18**

Premiership Top Four

2003/04	
2002/03	Man Utd, Arsenal *newcastle, Chelsea*
2001/02	Arsenal, Liverpool, Man Utd, Newcastle
2000/01	Man Utd, Arsenal, Liverpool, Leeds
1999/00	Man Utd, Arsenal, Leeds, Liverpool
1998/99	Man Utd, Arsenal, Chelsea, Leeds

Premiership Relegation

2003/04	
2002/03	West Ham, West Brom, Sunderland
2001/02	Ipswich Town, Derby Co, Leicester City
2000/01	Man City, Coventry City, Bradford City
1999/00	Wimbledon, Sheffield Wed, Watford
1998/99	Charlton, Blackburn, Nottingham Forest

Promoted to Premiership

2003/04	
2002/03	Portsmouth, Leicester City, Wolves
2001/02	Man City, West Brom, Birmingham
2000/01	Fulham, Blackburn, Bolton Wanderers
1999/00	Charlton Athletic, Man City, Ipswich
1998/99	Sunderland, Watford, Bradford City

Scholes, Silvest

S is for success, and also some of the star names that have helped *United* to achieve it over the years.

Full Name: Paul Scholes
Born: 16 November 1974, Salford
Position: Midfielder
Height: 170cm
Weight: 73kg
Transfer Fee: £0 (signed as trainee)
Previous Clubs: None

Of all the players who broke into the first team from the 1992 FA Youth Cup winning side, Paul Scholes is arguably the most naturally talented and technically gifted. In the 2002/03 season he came to terms with the position where Sir Alex really wanted him to play – just behind the main striker – and he responded with his best-ever haul of goals, including goals in six successive games in January 2003.

Paul has won almost everything there is to win in the game, certainly at club level. But medals on the international stage have eluded him so far, despite the many goals he has scored for England – including a memorable hat-trick against Poland in 1999.

It's a mystery why Paul misses out on the individual player awards. Not that the modest midfielder minds – he's happy to avoid all the attention and interviews!

Fan Chant
(to the tune of *"Kumbaya"*)
"He scores goals galore, he scores goals. He scores goals galore, he scores goals. He scores goals galore, he scores goals. Paul Scholes, he scores goals!"

Fun Fact
Sky TV's Soccer AM programme once broadcast the rumour that Paul is the proud owner of 33 cats. Not true!

Full Name: Mikael Silvestre
Born: 9 August 1977, Chambray-Les-Tours, France
Position: Defender
Height: 183cm
Weight: 83kg
Transfer Fee: £4 million
(from Inter Milan, Italy)
Other Previous Clubs: Rennes, Auxerre (both France)

After a shaky start to his United career, Mikael's name is now one of the first on Sir Alex's teamsheet every week. Although he plays at central defence for France, Mikael is more often seen bombing down the left flank for United, breaking forward from his full-back berth.

As well as being an accomplished defender, Mikael has also scored some vital goals for the Reds – none more so than his late headed winner against Leeds in March 2003 that kept United's Premiership title hopes alive. "I was about to take him off as he'd missed three chances," confessed Fergie after the game. "I'm glad I kept him on and he scored with the fourth!"

In December 2002 Mikael signed a new four-year deal that will keep him at United until June 2007. It looks like we'll be seeing a lot more of Mikael in the future.

e and Solskjaer

Fan Chant
(to the tune of *"Hey Mickey"*)
"Hey Mickey, you're so fine, you're so fine you blow my mind. Hey Mickey!"

Fun Fact
Mikael turned down a move to Liverpool because they wanted him to play at left-back instead of in central defence. He signed for United instead, and made his debut against Liverpool … playing at left-back!

Full Name: **Ole Gunnar Solskjaer**
Born: **26 February 1973, Kristiansund, Norway**
Position: **Forward**
Height: **174cm**
Weight: **73kg**
Transfer Fee: **£1.5 million**
(from Molde, Norway)
Other Previous Clubs
None

Ole Gunnar Solskjaer's place in United history was assured when his injury-time goal against Bayern Munich clinched the European Cup and historic Treble in 1999. But that's not the be-all and end-all of the Norwegian's achievements … he's done much, much more for Manchester United since joining the club as an unknown in 1996!

Ole almost left for Spurs a few years ago, but the manager stepped in to put a stop to the deal, not wanting to lose one of his prize assets. The prolific striker would walk into any other Premiership first team, but he chooses to remain loyal to United, and despite spending more time on the bench than he'd like, he's never heard to moan.

Ole's wife, Silje, gave birth to their second child, a girl named Karna, in March 2003, and the family look as though they're settled in Manchester for some time to come. Good news!

Fan Chant
(to the tune of *"Bobby Shaftoe"*)
"Who put the ball in the Germans' net? Who put the ball in the Germans' net? Who put the ball in the Germans' net? Ole Gunnar Solskjaer!"

Fun Fact
Ole psyches himself up for big games by singing Elvis Presley songs to himself!

Ferguson's other eleven

Like George Clooney's character in the film *Ocean's Eleven*, **Sir Alec Ferguson** is ably assisted by a team of individuals, each with their own specific role. But just who are these mystery men who surround Sir Alex on matchdays? Let's find out...

1 Rob Swire
First Team Physio

Rob is the man you'll see racing onto the pitch the instant one of our players goes down injured. As the club physio it's his job to get the players fit for the match, and to treat any knocks they pick up during the game.

2 Dr Mike Stone
Club Doctor

Dr Stone is on hand for serious injuries to players. Fortunately we don't get to see much of him during games. If we do – it's usually bad news. Amusingly, Dr Stone's mugshot mistakenly appeared on the back page of a national newspaper, when they printed his picture thinking he was Mike Phelan!

3 Carlos Queiroz
Assistant Manager

Previously the coach of the South African national team, Carlos joined United in summer 2002. The man from Mozambique made an immediate impact with his new ideas on how to train and prepare for matches. He's the fifth assistant manager at United, following on from Archie Knox, Brian Kidd, Steve McClaren and Jim Ryan.

4 Albert Morgan
Kit Manager

Albert has the job of getting all the players' kit to Old Trafford and laying it out before the stars arrive. He works hard to make sure everything is in the right place and in tip-top condition. Just don't remind him of the time when David and Ole ran out with "Beckam" and "Solksjaer" on their backs!

5 Alan Keegan
Stadium Announcer

Alan Keegan is the man with the microphone on home matchdays. Standing near the bench, he announces the teams before the game, and then the substitutions and the goalscorers' names during the 90 minutes. He also reads out special greetings messages and comperes half-time events like the lottery draw.

6 Dave Bell
Community Officer

Dave is the manager of United's Ladies' team, but on match day he's in charge of the ball-boys around the edge of the pitch. If the ball goes into the crowd, it's one of Dave's boys who will ask for it to be thrown back!

7 Alec Wylie
Assistant Kit Manager

Albert Morgan's able deputy and the man who helped Diego back into his shirt after that elaborate goal celebration against Southampton. The Uruguayan was having trouble putting his jersey back on after swinging it round his head, but cool and calm Alec came to the rescue!

8 Garry Armer
First Team Masseur

Garry tends to the aching muscles of the United squad, administering massages throughout the week and at half-time if needed. Garry took over from the long-serving Jimmy Curran, who retired at the end of the 2001/02 season.

9 Neil Hough
Reserve Team Physio

As the Reserves very rarely play on the same day as the First Team, Neil is usually on hand to provide important back-up to Rob Swire. Neil joined United from a rival Premiership club – we're not saying which one, though!

10 Tony Coton
Goalkeeping Coach

TC puts Fabien, Roy and Ricardo through their paces during the week, then helps them with their warm-ups before matches. Former City 'keeper Coton joined the coaching staff in 1998, helping Peter Schmeichel on his way to captaining United in the European Cup Final.

11 Mike Phelan
First Team Coach

Mike played for United under Fergie in the late 1980s and early 1990s. He came back to the club in the summer of 2001 to help out his old boss. Following a spell in charge of the reserves, he joined Carlos on the first team staff during the 2002/03 season.

RED PUZZLES

Backwards Quiz

Here's a chance to test your United knowledge, but be warned, there's a twist! Your task is to find the right questions for the answers, not the other way round. In other words, it works in the opposite way to a normal quiz. Best of luck!

1. Sheringham and Solskjaer
2. Glasgow
3. "The Theatre of Dreams"
4. Leytonstone in London
5. "Choccy"
6. The Vodafone logo, the Nike 'swoosh' and the United crest
7. £28.1 million
8. "The Baby-faced Assassin"
9. 166 yards by 76 yards
10. "Managing My Life"

Answers (or in this case, questions) can be found on page 60.

Squad Search

The names of twenty United players are hidden in the word-search below. Why not use a stopwatch and see how quickly you can find all the Reds?
(Remember to look in all directions!)

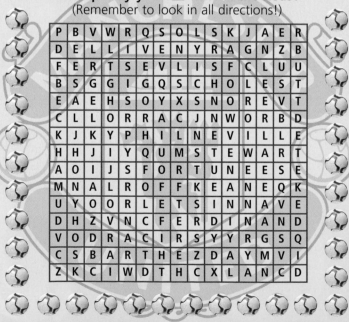

These are the players you need to find:

Barthez
Gary Neville
Phil Neville
Veron
Ferdinand
Beckham
Butt
Van Nistelrooy
Giggs
Carroll
Keane
Stewart
Scholes
Ricardo
Solskjaer
Forlan
O'Shea
Brown
Fortune
Silvestre

On the Ball

Across

1 Club captain and inspiration (3,5)

4 He's the Boss!(8)

7 French legend – we still sing his name (4,7)

9 Captained the team in the 1999 European Cup Final (10)

12 Wears the number 10. (3,10)

14 He won more medals than anyone in United history (5,5)

18 Paddy _____, Scottish legend (7)

19 The first great manager in United's history. (5)

20 Scored the winner in the 1985 FA Cup Final (9)

22 Bryan _____, Captain Marvel (6)

23 Serie A giants beaten in the 1999 Champions League semi (8)

27 Where we completed the Treble (3,4)

28 Brian _____. Former striker, now an Academy coach (7)

29 Robbo lifted this trophy a record three times as captain (2,3)

Down

2 Where United call home (3,8)

3 Won by the Reds in 1968 and 1999 (8,3)

5 German side beaten by two goals in a minute (6,6)

6 What the old First Division is now called (11)

8 Northern Irish superstar (6,4)

10 Ex-Red now bossing the Welsh (4,6)

11 Ottmar _____, manager beaten in the 1999 European Cup Final (8)

13 Bought from Norwich in December 1987 (5,5)

15 Norwegian hero who put the ball in the Germans' net (9)

16 Still the record goalscorer for United and England (8)

17 England captain and national hero (7)

21 Sir Alex's homeland (8)

24 Alan _____, who United fans love to hate (7)

25 Rio Ferdinand also plays for this team. (7)

26 Denis_____, King of Old Trafford (3)

United Nations
Your guide to Euro 2004

The 2003/04 season will be a long and hard campaign for some of **United's** best players … if they're lucky! Because once the dust has settled on the domestic season, there will be a fantastic international tournament taking place in Portugal. Here's our guide to **Euro 2004** and the **Reds** who might be there!

What's it all about?

Euro 2004 is the shorter name for the European Championships 2004. The tournament has been taking place every four years since 1960, pitting the best international teams in Europe against each other.

Where will it take place?

The tournament will be held in Portugal, the home nation of Luis Figo, one of the most expensive players in the world. Top Portuguese clubs include Benfica, Porto and the team that Peter Schmeichel joined when he left Old Trafford in 1999 – Sporting Lisbon. The legendary United goalkeeper helped Sporting win the Portuguese League in his first season, fresh from winning the Treble with the Reds!

When will it take place?

The tournament will start on 12 June 2004, with Portugal, as the host nation, playing the first match at the Antas stadium in Porto. The final will then be played 22 days later on 4 July 2004 at Luz in Lisbon.

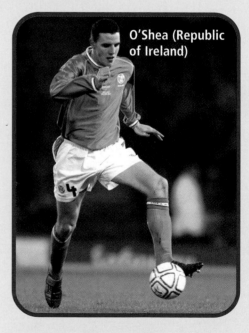

O'Shea (Republic of Ireland)

How many teams will be in it?

There will be 16 including Portugal, who qualified automatically as the host nation. Unlike the World Cup, the previous winners are not guaranteed a place in the tournament. Therefore France, featuring United's Barthez and Silvestre, had to play in

Beckham (England)

the qualifying round. This started in September 2002 with 10 groups of 5 teams – Ryan Giggs and Wales, for example, were in Group 9. The 15 teams that qualify with Portugal are the 10 group winners plus the winners of the 5 play-offs that are played between the runners-up in the groups. United star Paul Scholes scored when England beat Scotland in the Euro 2000 play-offs.

Will any United players be there?

Hopefully, yes! In fact, if all the United Nations qualify there should be enough Reds there to make up a team – with Barthez in goal; Silvestre, Rio Ferdinand, Wes Brown and Gary Neville in defence; Beckham, Scholes, Butt and Giggs in midfield; Van Nistelrooy and Solskjaer in attack. We've left out Roy Keane because he retired from international football after the last World Cup. And it should be obvious why Juan Sebastian Veron and Diego Forlan aren't there. They are both from South America, which has its own tournament for international teams called the Copa America. Quinton Fortune, meanwhile, plays in Africa's equivalent – the African Nations Cup. The World Cup is the only tournament that unites all the United Nations!

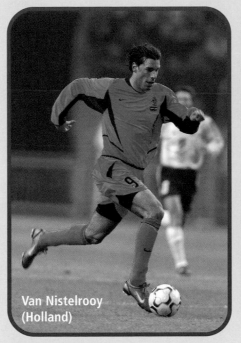

Van Nistelrooy (Holland)

Silvestre (France)

Cup two years earlier – what an amazing double! Another United goalkeeper, Peter Schmeichel, helped Denmark to win the European Championships in 1992. Denmark only entered the tournament because Yugoslavia were forced to pull out, but they defied all the odds to beat Germany in the final. They also beat Holland in the semi-final, thanks to big Peter saving a penalty from one of the world's greatest strikers, Marco Van Basten.

Have England ever won the tournament?

No, but they came very close in Euro 96, which was held in England. Gary Neville played in the early rounds of the tournament but missed out in the semi-finals when the Three Lions lost to Germany on penalties. Germany, who had played their group matches at Old Trafford, went on to beat the Czech Republic in the final at Wembley. The Czech side included a midfielder called Karel Poborsky who subsequently joined United.

How did England get on last time around?

Not very well! After qualifying through the play-offs, they were drawn in the same Euro 2000 group as Portugal, Romania and their arch-rivals Germany. Funnily enough, the Germany match proved to be the easiest

for England – they won it 1–0! Unfortunately England, then managed by Kevin Keegan, were knocked out after losing the other two matches 3–2, despite the efforts of David Beckham, Gary Neville and Paul Scholes, who scored after only three minutes against Portugal.

Best of luck to all the United players taking part in Euro 2004!

How many United Nations were there in the qualifying competition?

There were seven, as follows:

France : Barthez, Silvestre
Norway: Solskjaer
Holland: Van Nistelrooy
Northern Ireland: Carroll
England: Beckham, Brown, Butt, Ferdinand, P Neville, G Neville, Scholes
Wales: Giggs
Republic of Ireland: O'Shea

Have any United players, past or present, won the European Championships?

Yes. Fabien Barthez helped France to win the last one, Euro 2000. They had won the World

Giggs (Wales)

	Fabien Barthez (GK)	Roy Carroll (GK)	Gary Neville (FB)	Stock Market Crash:		Mikael Silvestre (FB)	
	2 £7 million	**3** £5 million	**4** FREE	**5** Lose £5 million	**6**	**7** £5 million	**8**

Team-B

50 Collect £5 million

Star Player Injured: 49 Lose £1 million

48

47

Ole Solskjaer (CF) 46 £7 million

45

Paul Scholes (CF) 44 FREE

Ruud van Nistelrooy (CF) 43 £9 million

The object of this board game is to follow in the footsteps of Sir Alex Ferguson and build your very own United team. You start with only £50 million to spend, but thanks to the club's successful youth academy, there are plenty of players you can pick up for free – including Beckham, Scholes and Giggs! Good luck!

Getting started: This board game is designed for two people. You'll need two dice (so you can roll from 2 to 12) and one marker each for the board – a button would be ideal.

Team sheets: Each manager will need a sheet of paper (lined A4 is best) and a pen or pencil. On the paper, write the following 11 positions vertically in this order: GK, FB, FB, CB, CB, WM, WM, CM, CM, CF, CF. The aim of the game is to write the name of a United player next to each of those positions, but you'll have to sign them first … so no cheating! Both managers start with a blank team.

Transfer fund: You can either use real money scaled down (e.g. 10 pence for £10 million) or just write down what you spend. Write 50 at the top of the sheet, then cross it off and write the new amount every time you lose or gain money. There should also be a sum of £100 million in the Bank. You'll collect £5 million from the Bank whenever you pass square 50.

Moving around: Both managers start at square 1. The manager rolling the highest score on the dice goes first. Each manager must then roll the dice and move their marker across the board by the number of squares shown on the dice. If you roll a double, you can have another turn straight away. If you land on an occupied square, you must move on one square. Play continues around the track – in other words, square 1 follows square 50. Every time you reach square 50, you collect £5 million from the bank to add to your transfer fund. If you land on a blank square after rolling the dice, your turn is over.

42	Juan Veron (CM) **41** £10 million	**40**	**39**	New Pitch Required: **38** Lose £4 million	Nicky Butt (CM) **37** FREE	Roy Keane (CM) **36** £9 million	**35**

	Win FA Cup:	Paul Tierney (FB)	New Kit Launch:		Wes Brown (CB)			Knocked out of Europe:
	10	**11**	**12**	**13**	**14**	**15**	**16**	**17**
	Gain £10 million	FREE	Gain £3 million		FREE			Lose £10 million

uilding

Player squares: You sign players by landing on their squares. If, for example, you land on Veron and your opponent has not yet signed him, then you can try to sign him for your team. If you decide not to buy the player, then your turn is over – your opponent is not permitted to buy him instead. If you decide to buy the player, check your transfer fund first to see if you can afford him. If it says Free, he's from the youth academy so you don't have to pay anything. If there is a fee, then you must first bid for the player by rolling the dice – a number equal to or higher than the fee means your bid is accepted. Deduct the fee from your transfer fund (if you're using real money, give it to the bank). Write the player's name next to his position on your team-sheet. If you have already filled the position, you can still sign the player and later sell him to your opponent. If you are running low on money, you can start your turn by offering to sell a player to your opponent in a transfer.

Transfer deals: If you land on a player who has already been signed by your opponent, you can try to buy him if you wish. If your opponent does not want to sell, the deal is dead and play continues. If your opponent is willing to sell, then you must negotiate a price. Once this has been agreed, the player is transferred to your team-sheet, while the agreed fee moves from your fund to your opponent's.

Game over: The winner is the first manager to complete his team with a player in each position. The game is also over if one manager (the loser) becomes bankrupt! Alternatively, you can set a time limit and see whose team is closest to being completed. If both managers have the same number of players, the winner is the one with the most valuable assets – i.e. the total value of players purchased plus the money remaining in their transfer fund.

vart	Kieran Richardson (WM)	Knocked out of FA Cup:	Quinton Fortune (WM)	New Sponsorship Deal:		Ryan Giggs (WM)	David Beckham (WM)
33	**32**	**31**	**30**	**29**	**28**	**27**	**26**
	FREE	Lose £3 million	£5 million	Gain £8 million		FREE	FREE

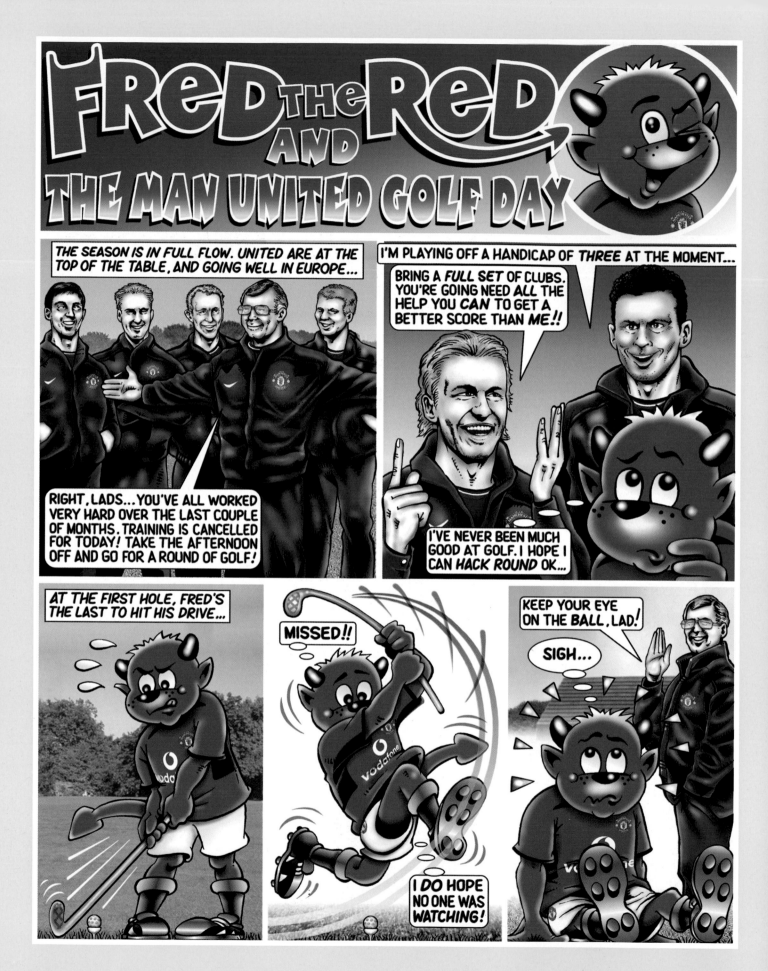

Answers to Puzzles

Who Said That?
(Pages 18–19)

1. Ryan Giggs
2. Wes Brown
3. Rio Ferdinand
4. Roy Keane
5. Juan Veron
6. John O'Shea
7. Ruud van Nistelrooy
8. David Beckham
9. Gary Neville
10. Fabien Barthez
11. Phil Neville
12. Paul Scholes
13. Ole Gunnar Solskjaer
14. Quinton Fortune
15. Diego Forlan

United by Numbers
(Pages 26–27)

Tall, short, old, young

1. (a) 37
2. (c) 19
3. (b) 6'3"
4. (a) 5'7"
5. (b) 48 years, 201 days
6. (a) Norman Whiteside
7. (c) 13st 12lb

Goals and glory

1. (a) 199
2. (c) Sir Bobby Charlton
3. (a) 36
4. (c) Ipswich Town
5. (c) 15 seconds
6. (c) 17
7. (c) 14

History and heritage

1. (b) 1878
2. (c) 10–0
3. (a) 135,000
4. (b) 15
5. (c) 15
6. (c) 6
7. (a) 14

Mixed bag

1. (c) 4
2. (a) 9
3. (b) 12
4. (c) 8
5. (b) 45
6. (b) £16 million
7. (b) 7

Red Puzzles
(Pages 50–51)

Backwards Quiz

Questions
1. Who scored United's goals in the 1999 Champions League final?
2. Where was Sir Alex Ferguson born?
3. What is Old Trafford's nickname?
4. Where does David Beckham hail from?
5. What is Brian McClair's nickname?
6. Which three symbols appear on United's shirts?
7. How much did United pay Lazio for Juan Sebastian Veron in 2001?
8. What is Ole Gunnar Solskjaer's nickname?
9. What are the dimensions of the pitch at Old Trafford?
10. What is the title of Sir Alex Ferguson's autobiography?

On the Ball
(Crossword)

Squad Search
(Word-search)

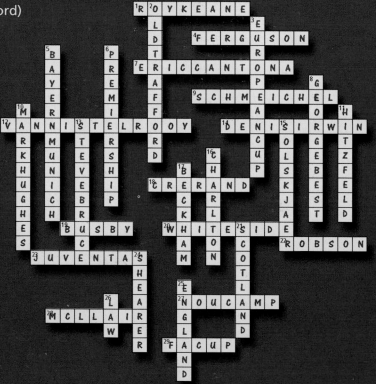